From
Poetry
To
Popcorn

Allan Ash
Canadian Poet

PublishAmerica
Baltimore

First printing

ISBN: 1-4241-0039-9
PUBLISHED BY PUBLISHAMERICA, LLLP
www.publishamerica.com
Baltimore

Printed in the United States of America

Take
A
Deep
Look
From
Within
Yourself
And
Your
Heart

Tells a tale you need to expel from truth

Introduction

How do you feel when poetry is able to stir up
Your heart to a level you have forgotten existed?
It may be bold, serene, strong, or other.
I believe a passion will unfold as you read further and further into
this second book of mine and you can experience
As I do, a renewed vision from within yourself

To

Borwen

My friend

Best Wishes

Allan Cox

, May 2009.

This book is dedicated to:

My greater power from above & you, readers of all ages who allow yourselves opportunities to enjoy a positive life, or try to keep an open mind that can be different. I guess a willingness to accomplish past the limits of time and
Mr. Ben Barkman who inspires a renewed assurance that there are good people living and caring about life; he has shown me a pure innocence for life that I rarely find in this world; it is definitely refreshing

A valley of beauty exists in front of you right now; reach out and grasp it with all of your might & by the hand of our almighty God, you will succeed

Special dedication to;
Mom & Dad, Bertha & Cyril Ash, Edmonton, Alberta
&
Marina & Diana Jimenez

Allan Ash
Canadian Poet

Contents

The papa bear down, syndrome

This resembles most males alike
As seen so many times before
In my day and days of yore

I am the Neanderthal male

Of power struggles
And deep brow expressions
As their sidekick wives struggle
To make all things right
In the minds of these futuristic men

I am the Neanderthal male

But heed the powerful tongue of
The female gender as
Greater is there powerful minds and words
Yet we are unable to adapt to this concept
And gripe at every chance we get

I am the Neanderthal male

Because we are male and built strong
Yet our pea-like brains simply
Put on an act that we are the only ones
Listening to ourselves chirp
I am the Neanderthal male

I have a waist to go and I will make it

Running on the treadmill of life
As the sweat pounds fall
To the ground
I am constantly reminded of
The hidden beauty
I have within the image
I see in front of me

And in time I know it will be worth it

Driven by determination and a pure
Sense to live a healthier life style
With every step I take
I run the pace of blinded
Determination and strive
To be the best I know and see
Within me

And in time I know it will be worth it

I alone determine my fate and heart's destiny
A gauntlet of sorts not a battle to be lost
Just a simple fact of life to be
All that I can be
And maintain a journey of purpose
With family in mind and enjoy it as long as I can

And in time I know it will be worth it

Breathe in
the breath of autumn

It's the sights and sounds that
I hear all around of nature in all of its
Splendors
And I can't help, but be awed with
The wonders it shares to us now
In its prelude to winter
With the echoing haunts of the forest's heart
So alive and busy with all it has to do
I see first hand as the little creatures
Of this land gather their food from
Nature as 'twas planned
Soldiering ants, passed by on their mission so fast
Steadfast and true
For they now sense the pre-immense
Of what shall come their way
A deep breath I now take
And engulf my lungs with this pure life
As I enlighten my thoughts once again
On the captivation this world holds on us
And finally, I bid farewell or adieu for a while
As I walk down this path through life once again
I now look at the time ahead when
Winter's blanket plans to leave us and awaken this land
Renewed with the sights, sounds, and the smells of spring to open
our hearts so we can do it all over again as we plan
Our next journey through the forest of time, life, and wondrous
dream-filled days to come and flood ours hearts with renewed
strength for passions in this precious world

It's a forest of dreams, but they're all mine

Listen to how the music captures
Your body into waves
Of movements like a long-awaited relief from
The stressful life we often lead
Brought back are those memories we had put
So far behind us, until another time & place
Drift into the electrifying trance it now holds
On you as you listen intently
With your feet and hands dancing there
As you sit in the audience of one's own living room
And enjoy it while you can
With no one to bother you for a while
And drift into the musical oasis of time
Straight into the forest of romance,
Passion, love and healing of one's
Mind and soul
Deeper and deeper you go as carefree
As the wind, you travel through the grove
Of splendid thoughts
Your mind travels farther and faster
Until you are lost into
Your very own little space of life
Now, while this moment lasts
Take a breath in so deep and exhale slowly
To allow your entire body
To float into emptiness, peace,
Relaxation and blissful inner strength
As a mellowing softness enters your body once again

Tap, tap there it goes again tap, tap

Looking out of my window
At home
I see the wind making the rain
Do an ever so gentle
Tap, tap on my windowpane
Right here in front of me
As if the rain were saying to me,
"Come on outside
And play with me
I'm here waiting just for you to
Jump and splash
In the puddles
Like we have done, so many times
Before."
Tap, tap goes the rain
Like it is getting
Impatient with me
Because I am not hurrying
Fast enough for him
Tap, tap as he sounds more and more
Anxious to see me now
So I grab my jacket, pants, rubber boots
As I rush to go outside
Still, as I open the door
I can hear him tap tapping
On my windowpane as I go outside to play
And now he is happy, because he is
Tap tapping on my rainwear
And I smile silently

The inner peace

The inner peace, carries us a
Long, long way to self-contentment,
Happiness, and joy
Replacing the bad storms in our lives
To a level our thinking patterns enjoy,
Such a blissful feeling obtained by a simple
Joyous emotion of enlightenment, positive
Thinking, and the way we live our lives
The harmony of a touching word
Said just at the right time
Gives a special meaning to our day
Leaving us with a butterfly feeling
Throughout our stomachs & a warmth full happiness
As we go into the tasks of another day
Welcome home our new inner soul to the world
As we now know it
And we can take it on the chin or on the sleeve
And wash away the gray times
That will be handed to us in every way.
It's comforting to know as we grow
A better feeling will explode inside of us
By just being a little kinder
To everyone we care for each and every day.
You, in what you have said & done, may not see it
Until a kindly jester comes your way, but it will
Play out no matter what you try to do
So be thankful for this very way
Think twice of what you do and say
For the path may be long that comes your way

Taming the tantrums from within

It's an obvious thing when a
Temper tantrum brews
Your eyes go all wacky
And the eyebrows do too
So evil and wicked, directed in place
At the ones who care and love you,
Yet you filled it with hate
Such a darling with malice
Written all over your face
And you stand there in front of us
And expect us to wait
While you vent your flaming anger
In haste, because things this time
Do not go your way
So you thought you would be
Bold enough
To speak in haste and hurt
All those that love you,
What a waste
Instead a freight train came barreling through
With unending shame
And no focus or fear of the people you hurt,
Just a greedy little person
Bent on getting your way
But, the lines have been drawn
And never fear for I am in control
Of what plays out today
And now you should fear the words you have spoken
Will come back and kick you in the rear

Her gentleness can tame us all

There's this special feeling, appearing
Every time you are near
To brighten the days
Of family, friends and your peers
You know just how
To make us feel
So close and dear
To your heart, thoughts, and deeds
So knowing this, stand tall
And proud
Because,
You are thought of
Each moment of every day
With respect, divinity, and grace
The versatility of your mind
Keeps us
A little humble time after time
In knowing
The person whom you are today
Will remain unchanged throughout
The ages
And knowing that you are loved
By family, friends,
And peers alike
Will remain an everlasting
Candle
In your memory
And
Theirs

At a snail's pace

That's how I see my world today in this very unique way
As I lie down on the grass and watch those great big
Clouds, glide gently by as they make images so beautifully in this
magnificent blue sky

At a snail's pace

My heart beats slow and contented, while I look deep into
The sky above and dream of tagging along with those fluffy,
pillowy, passions of white

At a snail's pace

That's how I see my life today and capture every moment in just
that very way, to stretch my mind beyond its capacity with endless
thoughts and visions of thankfulness and praise for our greatest
creator

At a snail's pace

With my arms outstretched and a great big grin, my eyes close
gently as I take this precious moment into my soul

At a snail's pace

Mother Nature surrounds me now with her echoing winds ready
to guide my path and all that stands within it
Will never want it to end, just keep it at a snail's pace

An Egyptian flair or was it that way

A mystical night from an era long ago
Rekindles such romances from a time of magical
Surroundings and wide-eyed admiration

Still the sands hide tales so deep within its soul
Of betrayals, love and hardships too painful
To remember, just like blinding sand storms
Which blocked out their visions

Yet we pass this off in awe of the wonders built
With such precision and know they will never to be replicated in
any other way, not today as if we ever could

Our hearts will be humbled with all that was given
By the workers, families and children alike
They never knew what it was like to be free of this
Pain in their everyday life

A lesson this way comes with a passionate plea to set your
Time to good use and you can see where it can lead,
For the splendor and its riches they amassed,
Did little in their time, but opened the encroachment
Of a newer timeslot filled with more and deeper greed

A new era of people have evolved with this passage
Of time, to know their time is spent well advised
Still we look at sandstorms as a nuisance
Not the heartburn held deep inside
A worn out land

Fate or faith upon your tongue

Think before you speak for your fate
Is sealed upon your tongue
Thus the journey may be long, so
Heed these words you say today,
They have a tendency to make you gray

The emotions spent in haste will lay in wait
Until a time of remembrance is upon your plate
And spill right back onto your lap from
Whence wrong words were said

It's now your thoughts, which you can change
To better ways to speak again of gentler taming
Of harsh words and reframing from what would
Have been said in haste

The end result is there to see as you set forth
A gentle breeze of thoughtfulness, caring too
And an honest look of concern, upon your face
Will melt away any fears this day at the one
You direct this message for

The storm was averted and your seas are calm
For doing what was right, not wrong.
Still you remain in charge of your life your path
And you made others feel better about
Themselves and others as well for this selfless moment

One against the elements

It remains instilled inside our souls as we
Venture forth grow older & deeper into thoughts
To ponder what life will bring our way
With each new dawning of a new day
For the road is paved with many hurdles
And many will make our blood boil or curdle
Yet, somehow we manage to trudge forward
With a clear purpose in mind
The focus of today will be, do not let the problems
Of yesterday creep back inside our thoughts,
And deal with new ones which occur today
Step not forth into tomorrow as so often we are guilty of
But enjoy the atmosphere we have around today
Before they too are gone
Accept what we no longer can change and for this
Your will shall remain intact and harmonious,
Elated and spontaneous with open arms and minds alike
For now the festive season is rapidly approaching with
Lights galore of many colors and music at every turn
Gleeful children ready to burst from their excitement as a very
special day approaches and the feelings were passed on to us as
well. Now we can feel it inside of our hearts and once again have
a chance to renew our friendships in life with friends, family &
ourselves
Deliriously we head off to many places to find that perfect gift for
those we love and to celebrate the birth of Christ with those
around us and travel to our favorite Church and our favorite pew
to hear of his birth once again

Faded paths, shadows of light

Haunt the soul of wisdom's blight
And draw you into a trance like state
Of divinity, and immeasurable peace of mind
As you look beyond the shadows of days gone by
And set your sights on what can be done to help humanity
Survive and prosper during their time and ours here on this
our precious God's-given earth

Faded paths, shadows of light

Precarious as this may seem you gleam in delight
With openness and heart felt thanks for walking this path
Back in time and not to burden you with woes
But cleanse your very soul so we can stand tall and bold

Faded paths, shadows of light

As we walk within our shadows and fragile pasts
Of casting themes, visions and dreams
We can feel the hopefulness of heart and life
From those that love us true and dear

Faded paths, shadows of light

As the shadows clear and the paths renew
A new revision this way unfolds and holds
The key to life and health without any fears
Or constant agony just living a wonderful life inside
And allows the beauty from within to unfold

The mist of morning, when darkness calls

The mist of the morning and the dew on the grass
Are like cleansing tears of relief from above
Sent to us
With a very special message in mind
To all he loves here on earth
And those that have already passed on
A kind reminder
For the path we walk in life
Is for him, through him
And always, with him
A new beginning starts
Here today as you continue
On your life's path
Now the freshness you inhale
Leaves a gentleness once again inside
While the people around you see such
A warm and calming spirit
Emanating from your smile
And this will carry good feelings
For all today and forever
Finally when the evening has past
And you are home for the night
Know he will be with you
As you lay again in bed to sleep
In peace and comfort with his spiritual
Arms holding you tight

Hidden so deep
God reached for her hand

Inside the forest of confusion
Lies an untapped heart afraid to blossom
Hidden from view for such a long time
Into the darkest recesses of her faithful soul
Always willing to step aside and let another
Opportunity for love slip her by
And fade into a fleeting memory of what could have been
The sanctity of her own thoughts
Are muffled as she clamors in her heart
To be free of the fear to move ahead
And seek true happiness with the Lord's guidance.
She wants to let her heart beat strong with independence,
assurance, and hope to move forward
All she needs is a little help from God and his faithful Angels
So, with a gentle nudge and a firm hand on reality they
Trudge though her forest together to help set a heart free
Although many obstacles
Arose from the thickets along the way
They are overcome one by one with the help
Of our almighty God
Now the darkness is starting to grow brighter the farther
They enter her hidden recessed heart and a glimmer
Of hope is within her reach for her own reality to view
And her outstretched hands they see in front of them are a
testament of God's almighty power as she takes that very first step
into faith's holy path and awakens a new
Beginning of her life refreshed, uplifted
And her focus clear

Conditional love, unconditional love

Conditional love
It is a fact that's terrible,
But so very true
We live in a time and age of
Sad beliefs, lost souls, money greed
And conditions put on almost everything in life
Including love, compassion, faith,
Family, church values
And friendships

It appears for some there is
Nothing sacred anymore and the passion
For a perfect life doesn't exist
Except in fairy tales and our fantasies
Or visions as we did see them when
We were very young and naïve

What has robbed the soul of its true destiny?
And the belief there is unconditional love
Inside our hearts if we let it out
With a feeling more wonderful
We just need to stop and feel it inside of our hearts
The way our Mothers raised us to believe in ourselves
And in our humanity as we know it

Search deep within yourself for the good you have
And amazing things will truly unfold
Tides of change are all around
We only have to accept them

A time for reflection & thankful hearts

Take this time to celebrate, as Christ's birth approaches
And remember the coming of the child into
Our lives to cleanse our souls and forgive us for
Our many transgressions and sins
Rekindle your heart with a love so strong and pure,
Sing proud for the strength of the Lord is within us all
Devote time to say thank you for all he has done
And the many paths he brings our way
We are the reason he came to us
Look beyond the path we have chosen and
Return to his path & his spiritual fulfillment.
Look not at what Christmas has become for many,
But at how the message was set forth
In the beginning
This precious gift, the Christ child was born and he lay
Sleeping in a Manger with Mary, Joseph, three wise shepherds,
angels and the animals
For the glory of the Lord is among us this day
And forever more
The sanctity of his vision will always remain
We are the reason he suffered and died,
Through our Lord we will share his
Glorified message throughout the ages and pass
Onto others the true meaning of Christmas
As it was meant to be handed down
For his strengths are the beginning and the end
Blessed be the power and the glory of our
Gracious Lord And savior
Jesus Christ, Amen

Babysitting your heart

Doesn't give you the cause of the pain or the outlet to
Repair it. That, you have to find within yourself

Remember your values and how they came about

Search your thoughts on how the message came to you
How did you come to this conclusion?

Remember your values and how they came about

Compromising ideas set this path you're on
In motion and stumbling in the darkness
Doesn't help to clear those visions

Remember your values and how they came about

From whence this came captures your
Frame of mind leaving you with
A most exhausted feeling & zero patience

Remember your values and how they came about

When an overpowering reality returns to your brain
Always remember, it's you that can make
The necessary changes happen

Remember your values and how they came about

Darling child, my heart of life

A new year has arisen on this your Birthday
We are a part of your special celebration
Of life with a birthday party
Made especially for you
Awesome gifts you have yet to unwrap
And to see your friends who
Surround you this day
It's this incredible way about you
With that brilliant morning smile,
So welcomed with each dawning morn'
That makes you so special to us
Those tender gentle eyes that look
Upon us every day
And a heart full of love, hope, & life
Are welcomed from you as well
Beginning each day with the way
You look at all of us
There's so much love and so many caring thoughts
Projected from your eyes and smile
You make us feel warm inside
To be as special as you are
To all of your friends
Know that you are loved
And respected by your peers
And cared for by all who love you
This is why special wishes are
Sent to you
You are worth every one

Friends forever, friends for life

It all started from a chance meeting when
They were placed together in a home environment
as tots. In a school beginning at a wee age
Such as four or five maybe teens or adults.
However it happens,
You can sense it from the start
A special bonding of the heart,
What you both feel inside is
A new best friendship growing
So you plan many things to come
Like sharing secrets
Nobody else knows
Talking about silly things
And giggling over and over
About sometimes nothing at all
Forever friends and never far away
From each other's thoughts
This holds the deepest passion
Of all
And in the years to come
The bond is so strong there is absolutely no
Way of breaking it apart
There will come many challenges, obstacles
And sometimes pain, but
You both will survive the challenge
And learn valuable lessons along the way
Because the bond of friendship
Is as thick as family
And this will never change

Enough is enough

How much willpower can
A mind endure
Or take
Before it finally
Explores
New avenues to expel
Its distaste
A chore at best,
But fleeing the nest
Is
A copout at best
When coping and listening
Seems a waste of time
Unless you are willing
To make a difference
In this your lifeline
Spell out the harmony you
So often seek
Without harboring thoughts
Of deceit
Shortcomings are not far
From home
You only have to admit
The fault zone
From
One's comfort zone
And anger
Has no place here

It's a powerful voice that sings
or speaks

If you let it or a fading whisper
To help you fail
Because of your fear
To succeed
Or a zone you created
In your mind
Doesn't sell your dream
In your voice
To anyone, but who you are.
Dream the desire
And learn as you go with the flow
There is nothing you cannot
Achieve
When you put your heart
Into it
From the time the umbilical cord
Was severed you have
Challenged many doors
To get to where you are
At this present time in your life
Challenges are supposed to be rewarding,
Daring, fun, and give you the sense
Of accomplishment
And most gratifying are the opportunities
You did try which were offered to you
Because somebody believed
In you

From poetry to popcorn

Who said poetry and popcorn would not mix
After all, it is a quick fix to satisfy your cravings
Of the taste buds on your tongue and one's mind to
Solo adventures into words of poems which brings back
Reality of seconds, hours, days, months
And years so Vivid, while indulging your new-found views
So deep within a poetry verse, phrase or book
That has you captivated intently. Now listen to this very statement
of mind, my heart as you so cleverly reach for another handful of
savory extra-buttered popcorn
Your eyes would not miss a second
As the words melt into your utmost thought of thoughts
So engulfed at what you are reading you dare not take time
To breathe for fear the moment is lost from where you have taken
yourself. And its passion is unfolding to bring you back. Still your
hand again reaches for that awesome taste
That blends so well with poetry you so want to enjoy.
Ah, it's fate, realize what you see inside these poems.
What brought these two together? And the aroma in the air
Is so contagious it automatically has the hand
And the mind once again, seeking its target
As the eyes read on in knowing that at the close of the poems you
have just finished
You can savor the flavors from your mind
And to your lips while looking for another special time and place, to
reunite them both with impending expectations
Of an encounter as marvelous as the first, a blending so unique it
stands to reason they belong together

Straight from the heart

Flows a lifeline so true, nobody
On earth can cease its true course

Straight from the Heart

Comes solid wisdom echoing the knowledge
Gained from past experiences and journeys

Straight from the Heart

The arrow of love enters its new partner
And starts a wealth of romance and passion

Straight from the Heart

Sounds the adoration for living life as a free spirit
And passing on its free will to you as they go

Straight from the Heart

A driven destiny withstands the test of time and love
Abounds even through hardships, doubts & fears

Straight from the Heart

It passes the deepest trust onto other loved ones who
Have crossed this very same path before
And they know what they have to do
To continue this trek

Tempting as it is, I'll stay the course I'm on

A biscuit of sweetness enters the race
To deliver a message of power and grace
Until it is right in front of your face
And you will falter and hide
Into the bosom of lies

Tempting as it is, I'll stay the Course I'm on

A balance of power, evil as sin wants to gather
You up and promise all things from the stars
To the moon and other benefits thrown in
As a twist to reel you in

Tempting as it is, I'll stay the Course I'm on

Thou do try and try so very hard, but there is no need
To carve a sense of false decency inside my brain,
Because I know your evil, evil games
On this your train and I will stay my course
Of my decency as valor, chivalry will never die
Not ever, in these mine eyes, if I were blind

Tempting as it is, I'll stay the course I'm on

I think not how you play your games I will remain
In my true frame of mind and be my God's best friend
For what you ask is temporary, yet what I seek is everlasting

Look not upon this body of mine

Before I capture and intertwine your feeling of good
Inside my mind and rape what you hold back not
Of me to intertwine between my thighs know it is for you alone I
think

Your fear is greatest to me

I now can pick at random and choose a corruption of your
Good, so you may never be in control, at random is what
I do best this is my way so you can never rest.

Your love for Christ is stronger than I

Except God interferes at
Every chance you are such a fool at heart
Because your so-called precious God is in your heart

Your love for Christ is stronger than I

Divinity & self-control with God's help will make you very
Bold to challenge the devil and his fraudulent fears

Your love for Christ is stronger than I

When all things are said & done God's willpower this way
Shall win over, a small battle this time, but it makes you stronger
each and every time. Thank you so incredibly much for sending
your only son

My quivering lips help to shed my tears

As they fall one by one,
On my pillowcase
I have to take
A reflective moment
Back to the sermon
I heard from a pastor recently
My eyes are wrapped
Into those thoughts
Thinking to myself there will
Always be a message from God
To comfort all who need it
My tears seem to say
Goodbye to the way
I once was,
And welcome back the
Actual person
That is loved even though
I was not recognized
For the pain I suffered.
Those shedding tears
Release such pain
It is hard to contain myself
Yet, I feel this presence
By my side
Which makes me feel
Worthwhile
Inside

Broken and in pain
I'm at your mercy

It's my time, that's right, look at the color of my
Kneecaps, shoulders, legs & thighs, as they hurt,
They are skinned and peeling from my fall.
Blood Trickles down as my eyes fill with tears
That flow upon my soft facial cheeks.

Mom and dad are by my side
Where they will leave an everlasting
Effect upon my, well you know my
Pride, do not say it loud
So embarrassed I am, the only
Thing left to do is
Weed out my complaints to better relate
My wishes and save face,
I bet you thought all I would say is
Cry
I'm only a kid, how can this be
I was invincible and still I bleed
As at this age I do believe
My ups and down are bouncing me around
With a path not determined or found
Until I can look back at what was had and yes
I admit it, my good youthful days
Will eventually be gone by the wayside
Of which I was never a slave
Now I'll return in a little while to be
A kid just having fun
And while away endless hours of play
With my friends

Is it a crime
to be a passionate parent?

Protecting your children is bred into you
As a parent your mind plays
All kinds of tricks on you,
So you
Stick with your decisions
Even though
It may be tuff
And they fight it
All the way
As they huff and
They puff
And our children
Feel stifled and stuck
In a rut, as they say.
But, they are so frail
In my eyes
And streetwise
They are not
It may be 4 blocks
From our home that
They walk, but to me,
Every step is a mile and a half
With so many factors at risk
All the way
I'd rather pull out my hair or
Become completely
Grey
Than to have any
Harm happen to them

Many graces
much to be loved

The way she looks, her smile so bright
It makes it just a sheer delight
To want to capture and to hold this
Innocence I now behold
In front of me
The captivating way she talks with such
Intense adoration for the simple things in life
There is an aura about her and
A wonderful feeling for jest in this life
A mother's influence I can see in her
With mannerisms and charms
That can melt a
Heart so fast, no one stands a chance
To back away from her romancing eyes
As her gentleness unfolds
An audience awaits her wants and desires.
Because of the youthfulness in her dainty fingers
It adds a splendid flair
As she beckons you near
This so elegant lady I see
Right here
In front of me can simply ask
And yes, I too
Would give my heart
If called upon to do so and treasure
Each and every moment so
Gather up this time with her and
Let a new passage of time begin

Knowing the difference is the right thing to do

Even when the feeling to proceed is
Not quite the way others perceive
A perception from you to be
We have to take a stance
Or a time-out so we to can recognize
Our further needs and develop
A better feeling for what we see, say,
And do to influence decisions
We have to make
In front of those peers,
Family, friends
And God most of all
A single moment
Viewed at the wrong time
Can be mistaken by the people
For fear
Of something gone very wrong.
The eyes can be deceived into
Believing what they just saw
Was a shock to them and
Seeing isn't always believable
But the human instinct inside
Scrambles to deny
Such thoughts
And argues with itself
Until an agreeable solution
We can comprehend
Comes to mind
A resolution of thought

At first glance, a second chance to review

I have to proceed with the path
I was on because the purpose
I saw in my eyes
Was all wrong
There is a moment of craziness
Entering my brain
As the magician vows to stun us
With his display
Of mastery and trickery
His posture sure and true
While the crowd
Watches his sleight of hand
Stunning and eerie his display
For the dark side is at hand
And he carries on
Without flinching a muscle.
The audience is in silence
As an object disappears right
Before their very eyes
And with the awes of approval
From his captive audience, shows
He has accomplished his deed
And before they have a chance to blink
He continues on with a new performance
Not yet tried, but the atmosphere is right
To gather again in amazement
The glimmer and sparkle in those eyes
As it feeds his soul to the abyss of
Continued success and drama on the dark side of magic

From passion, paradise unto forever

Though many of life's journeys have their ups and downs
And from this way and that way we are pulled along
Yet, we remain strong in the belief from our head
Down to our feet, it's our hearts that speak
More of what we seek
And beyond our understanding for a while
Like a lightening bolt the mind sets its visions
For us to once again take that extreme risk or heart-filled chance
and get swept away by the uplifting sail of freedom or a train of
thought so intense, passionate and deep into paradise's embrace. It
pulses though our veins as we speak out loud in the silence of our
comfort zone, even if in the accompaniment of family, friends,
acquaintances or peers.
As we gently land into forever's embrace
And alight safely upon its bosom of peace and contentment
A sigh expels from inside one's own depth and reveals
Yet again a renewed ambition to carry on just as if it was the first
time all over again and again.
Carry forth this feeling with robust enthusiasm because
Of what you have sought for so long is now attained forever. Step
into the abyss of yet another path as you move forth into your next
chapter of life as it is meant to be and regale at the triumphs left
behind especially those failed, tested, & proven without a shadow
of a doubt to work,
By this I mean 'twas by far worth every tear, anguishing thought
and long hours of soul searching to find answers of growth. Least
we forget those growing pains we shall always experience which
we have shelved for far to long.

A steadfast knight and his steed of strength

Set forth to gather his bride for life
And gather he did by his strength
Of deeds and his mighty-fine brain
With so much ambition to fend for
The lives for those he did need
To protect, help, and preserve
Their virtues no matter the cost.
For this is his cause
As he ventures forth
Committed to this way
He stands steadfast and tall.
Though his life
Was as normal as anyone's can be
He set forth to gather provisions
He did need.
To present himself to others
As a worthy catch
To the one he wanted to hold
Close to his breast.
A pillar of hope, truth, & respect
This knight in shining armor was calm
Collected so fearless and unmoving
Before anyone knew it
With his marvelous abilities
He waited to bait his opponents
One by one as they lay in wait
But his true passion was his Queen as
Magical moments
Haunt their minds as their lips first kissed

Promising moments can crush the heart

Or maybe not!

All this over a cup of tea as your heart
Does a little pitter-patter
Of anticipation

Or maybe not!

Everything happens for a reason as
We journey through this
Our life's path
Or maybe not!

Whether good, bad or other matters at hand
Aren't ours to plan, yet we continue
To believe they are

Or maybe not!

Just when we believe we have the upper hand
And start to feel at ease our path
Is suddenly altered

Or maybe not!

A long-awaited dream or wish had come to life
And set us up for great things ahead
As we dare to plan

Or maybe not!

How humbling a feeling it gives to us

As we sit in our favorite pew at church
Or even in the solitude of our abode
As we listen to the sermon at hand
And feel the presence of the all mighty
Lord and his angels at our side
To wash away our faults, sins & shortfalls
And echo in a newfound hope & thirst for
All to adhere to once again
As is his mighty plan.

Humbly remember all we are given
Is by his very hand alone
Even though we may have worked
Very hard to achieve success
It is without a doubt by his almighty hand again
In an instant can remove all we have achieved
And cast it out yet bring us to our knees
As we gather our thoughts and come to terms
With elements far beyond our control

Into a mirror we only have to look and glance
Deep into our soul of thoughts
And ask are we following the right path?
Or are we stumbling about in the dark?
Can you feel it? Are you ready?
It is never to late to start anew, refreshed
In the belief we can make a difference to those
We hold so dear and those around us
One step at a time is all that it takes & do jump in.

God's Cerebral Palsy Wonders

So we can understand not to take, but to receive
In faith a pure understanding that it could be you or me
In this very same position, or a co-worker,
Family member, maybe even another we love.
Go about your business and enjoy this human race,
As we believe it was meant to be.

It is through God we shall kneel
And these special chosen ones with Cerebral Palsy
They do not understand, but they will succeed
And they too will know why they have been chosen to live this
way, even though their wish is an easy simple timetable
Of understanding, yet hardly anyone takes the time to hear

Stop what you are doing and bend
Those knees as you retire for the evening
And ask for forgiveness for your selfishness
Your greed, but do not give sympathy just empathy,
Understanding to those worse off than you or I
Ponder your thoughts for those with afflictions
While you stand so free to move about
As others rely on you

For the Lamb of God touches each and every
Soul of those brave hearts
Be it Spastic, Athetoid or Ataxic
For stiff and difficult movements, involuntary and
Uncontrolled movements or disturbed sense of balance and depth
perception, they are all God's beautiful children

And in all likelihood it may come true

Passion, hopes, dreams and expectations
Haunt many moments throughout
Our lives as we move ahead

And in all likelihood it may come true
And who knows?

Setting a steadfast direction with which
We can advance towards our dreams
Just down this path we lead

And in all likelihood it may come true
And who knows?

A drifting pattern emerges from our minds
Setting us to find its final end

And in all likelihood it may come true
And who knows?

But as we are human and can be at fault
Though many of our paths for which
We have chosen

And in all likelihood it may come true
And who knows?

Just believe in yourself with God's almighty power and all
Things will prevail because he knows it will

Tender moments opened wide

I hold out these arms for the most
Tender of moments
And block
All the bad there is in this world
Just to savor
These moments with you
Enclosed
So deep within my bosom

Say, my heart is open wide

And open the inner-
Most visions
You have held so deep
So hidden
Yet burst with excitement
As you begin to explore incredible
Realms

Say, my heart is open wide

It's
A beautiful moment when
Taking care of business
The restorations of beliefs in one
For far to long have been ignored
And how can you believe in this
Wondrous development?
Minds can concur

Flowers, gardens and Roses

A deep breath expels from within me as I stroll my garden of
renewed budding life. With the blanket of snow now long lifted, the
ever so softening of the ground brings back
A well-known feeling that just around the corner
Brilliance for these tempting eyes again awakens
Yet, before we know it an awaking day shows
The newness of the early morning dew bringing a sense
Of a new beginning to this our life and wonder about
All this beauty offered here within and you can
See it unfold
Ahhs of pleasure expel from me as I open my eyes
Quickly embodying everything I can see at first sight
This I relive as if for the very first time again
I now see the beauty produced from a single seed
And I feel so peaceful once again right here & right now
The aromas of the flowering buds burst forth
With their Excedrin of explosive captivation
Drifting throughout & calming all that enter this way
I am lost in this my Garden of Eden
Yet as I explore further & further
Inside this special place
I see and hear the sights and sounds of the bees
As they seem to bounce so effortlessly
From flower to flower
The sweet songs generated by the Robin redbreasts
Sparrows & nature as they sing their glorious song to their new
born and everlasting mates
Take a deep breath inside can you feel it? It's renewed life, as we
know it

They ask nothing in return

As we depart from home I glance back at my front window
And there appearing through the sheers are these
Lonesome eyes peering right through my very soul
Piercing my heart as he tilts his little head
Wondering why I am leaving him all alone
And my heart breaks, as his sad eyes stay etched
Inside my mind
As the day passes and the evening approaches
My thoughts are drifting back to the images I felt
As I left for work and I stop into the pet store
And buy some treats for this precious soul.
As I pull into the driveway I see the curtain
Move and there appears my faithful pet with his
Tail a-wagging
His greeting is so real as I open the front door
And he walks so proud beside me now and utters
Not a sound, then he goes back over to his favorite area
And watches me some more and I feel safe.
With the dishes done we set off for a run,
I can tell how happy he is by
The way he bounces alongside of me
And that tongue of his hanging there flopping
From side to side, I can't help but chuckle
To myself as this sight is too wonderful to pass up.
With the run all done and we are all cleaned up
For the night I lay in my bed to read a little before
Retiring for the night then a head pops up right by my side as he
checks to see that I am all right, now his head goes back down as
we say goodnight and I turn off the light

I am at a loss for words

Here I sit ever so quietly taking in all this
Beautiful country scenery when into my view
From the clearing right in front of me walks
A fawn, oh how splendid this creature is
And I move not a muscle for fear of scaring
This precious thing
My heart stops for a moment as she starts
To move just a little closer to me
Unfazed by my presence she continues
To move around without a care in this world
I watch as she moves about then she stops and
Her head turns and her ears are now attentive
To something I cannot hear
Then with a playful move she walks right
Up to within two feet of me
My heart is beating so fast at this magnificent fawn
The way she looks at me tempting me to run
With her and play, I am in awe
I take my hand and ever so slowly reach out
To see if I can have her come closer
She stands with such poise and caution at first
I stop and proceed no more
Just as I am about to move my hand closer
She gets ready to run, I stop and wait to see
What she will do next
And without warning I feel the coldness
Of her nose right on the back of my hand
Our eyes meet for a split second
Then off she bounces back into the thickets

This way

Here a kiss I plant on you
And this shall tell you true
Of how my love is waiting here
Just for you
In every essence of its meaning
Though said in many fashions,
Forms, and phrases
They long to gather you up inside
To while away endless hours
In tranquil peace
By each other's side
To dream of things yet to come
And capture magical moments
As we peer directly
Into each other's eyes
And close out the world for now
A renewed nervousness enters in
As rekindling thoughts of love
Flutter throughout our hearts
And our minds are swimming
With anticipation of all there is in store
In the weeks, months & years ahead
Ours hands now united
With a path straight and true
We take that first step to plan
A secret rendezvous for two
And our emotions we no longer
Can hide

Velvet Angel hear my cries

Cry out oh heart of mine
For I seek another chance
And in desperation I seek it
Not that way
And yet, to escape what
I fear
Is holding me here
For my comfort is shadowed
All alone
I feel shattered
And ever so empty inside
Hear my cries and feel my tears
Help me deal with this
Internal loneliness of what if's
And the longings that are constantly
In my ears, mind, & thoughts
The visions I seek are all too consuming
Do listen to me now
With these longings I want so much
Can I change what I feel so strongly?
Do I actually want to continue on in this way?
Angels hear the screams of frustrations
And guide me back to somewhere
If time could be altered
By our minds' thought processes
Dear we step into this path
And take that chance
To do things differently

The warm sun on a beautiful summer's day

Has taken me away to my garden of hope and peace,
Tranquilities embrace, I am now surrounded by
No sights and sounds of the urban noise
Just the pleasantries of nature's workers
As the gathering of nectar and food carries on
A slight breeze brushes over the flowers and trees
Setting a wave of contentment to flow throughout
Every leaf
The warmth of the sun has been placed all around
Allowing the garden to grow more and more beautiful
With each and every breath it now takes
Such fragrant aromas bring forth the calmness
I seek and I am lost to its beauty.

Embracement of patterns flows all around
As the leaves, bees & other flying insects sing their songs,
I stroll about my garden I am empty of thoughts
Except for the beauty that surrounds me now
My heaven on earth & my Garden of Eden are
Beneath my feet my soil of life so to speak
Ahh, the birds in their playful flight go this way
And that way so elegant and strong
Though if it were true I too would tag along just for a while
To feel the freedom and the wind on my face
The ducks and the geese with their families in tow
Paddle along in a unison flow, so proud they all look
As I gather in this view and a smile comes on my face
As I am again renewed

Wilderness speaks
& the waterfall roars

Breathtaking. I am lost for words as the trail has
Opened up to show its splendor and the trickle
Of the water just off to the side I can hear
The sounds of a waterfall offering
Up its splendid roar, the mist it releases
Shows a rainbow overhead makes my heart skip a beat
For to see all the greenery, trees, & scenery everywhere
I view. I am taken aback and remember this is
God's hand and his plan for this area of the land
How marvelous, flamboyant, robust and so lush
As I enter in, overwhelming emotions well in my eyes
For this beautiful sight simply wants me to cry
And release hidden feeling so deep inside
Of how happy I am to have had this chance
Just for a moment to glance on something
So uplifting a healing of such and
The gleam of the water from the sun's rays
As it flows so peacefully on its never-ending
Journey to replenish this land
Above the waterfall I spot with my eyes a
Golden eagle with his head held high
And his wings spread out gathering up the
Warmth of the sun as the rays pour down
Yet, in from of me by the rill I see several
Species of birds singing and gathering food
What a sight I never want to leave
For this tranquility is unbelievable
As I journey past these wonders of life I will
Never forget this sight etched in my mind

A whimsical tale
of utter nonsense & silly words

Silly isn't it to be this way, but you have to admit
It's the greatest way to start the day and dream of
Being a princess with long flowing hair
Or a little boy just wearing hockey gear
Anxiously waiting for mom and dad to leave for the day
So you can jump, scream, run, and play in muddy puddles,
Catch frogs, tadpoles and roll in the grass
And have those bright green knees from what else
But the grass you silly goose
No cares no worries and talk to yourself about any
And everything there is to think of
I'm feeling giddy and so silly
I want to pick my nose and put it on my wall
Or splash all day in the bathtub and write soapy messages
On the walls as my fingers shrivel up like cauliflowers
Even better yet to have a water balloon fight with
All of my friends
So many things are rushing through my brain it's like a
Freight train dropping little hints here and there
Dizzy and happy at best I will never grow up for awhile
But for now I just want to clown around
Jump on my bed throw my clothes in the air and write
Messages on notepaper and stick them all over
My room and throughout the house,
Out of the corner of my eye I see the confused
Look on the face of my pet as he stands a good distance
Away from me, this would be fun to do
What's stopping you?

Her eyes are not blind to caring

Though the days may pass and go unnoticed
To most of us, still certain eyes take in stride
What we know stays inside with her as
She continues onto her work load day by day

Her eyes are not blind to caring

I can't even imagine let alone fathom
Or hope to achieve the same, while she plans
Another of her hectic days it doesn't escape
The kindness displayed, be it very seldom,
Short lived or played out or underplayed.

Her eyes are not blind to caring

Still with unbending efforts we know from her heart
A longing to be the same like us and
Straight from the heart
Now watch as the walls continue to fall and her
Gentleness prevails and unwinds with this God-
Given day we now have a special gathering for her
Today, so with her family & friends here this day
We do now boast as we declare
You are very special to us
And always will be

Her eyes are not blind to caring

So you see, it is the greatest time of your life

Just the chance at being yourself is a healthy and so
Vivacious, as that of the aroma made by homemade bread
Straight from the oven where everyone want the heels

So you see, it is the greatest time of your life

No cares, no worries, no problems tells a tale in itself
And it feels as natural as grandma making homemade
Chicken soup for us when we are at home sick with a cold

So you see, it is the greatest time of your life

The stories and the tales our grandparents have told to us
Although repeated so many times before sets a path in our
Brains and this too, is as natural as peanut butter and jam
On homemade bread and toast

So you see, it is the greatest time of your life

To experience hardships in life are only a heartbeat away
Giving us a look at life's awkwardness's and unique
Outlooks of things we say we will change as we become adults is
as natural as homemade apple pie

So you see, it is the greatest time of your life

Experiencing life to the fullest is as natural as roast beef, mashed
potatoes, & the trimmings after church on Sunday morning with
family & friends and may God bless us all

The honor is all mine and you know it

A gleam in her eyes was entrusted to me as I read
A few verses from this poetry you see
Her excitement so pure, fresh and rewarding
I humble myself to tell of its coming

And you know it

With anticipation I read further & to envision an
Audience where I too can carry on with the
Expressions I feel with these words I now write
And listen to the wisdom she applies right here tonight

And you know it

The eyes of her expressions, passions of understanding
Leaves me feeling renewed with my life to carry on farther
and deeper in thought, I can hardly contain myself with my
thoughts to write more yet I know you will not be bored

And you know it

A brief encounter is all that it took and thank God, I will
never forget her look for the innocence is a given, you
know it so well as do I and the rest of this verse I needn't
reply for it speaks for itself without borders or bounds

And you know it

Quivering passions still remains

As the soft, warm, and enticing breath within the two of us expels
such fantasies with which we lure the other's embrace to open
feelings welling inside
Oh how my heart's alive with fire and thirst

We both dive into this with fluttering feelings from the heart
And care not to delve into the future of confusions of what if's or
maybe's
Oh how my heart's alive with fire and thirst

Quivering inside with excitement for a new-found love I dare to
hold these rough hands of mine on her magnificent, gentle, loving
& innocent face
Oh how my heart's alive with fire and thirst

Ever so slowly I bring my face and lips passionately close to hers
and feel the heat within us flow freely as her head tilts back ever
so slightly as that of time-lapsed photography longing for a
romantic kiss
Oh how my heart's alive with fire and thirst

With eager anticipation while her mouth opens slowly in an
enduring quest as doth mine of a divine kiss planted
sweetly. Her eyes drifted from my eyes to my lips and far
beyond the realms of controllable lust as was I. Yet,
the blood abounds upon her crest and a touching of lips
long to gather and intertwine

Bumps in the road
the growing pains of life

Begin as soon as you start to crawl, walk, & talk so,
Be it as it may, there will be many delays
As you stumble through your journeys, paths and hurdles.
Incredible is the life set there before you to capture all
In good time as marveling thoughts block your visions
For a minute, an hour or many days
As everyone watches you grow it's your time to shine
Today, tomorrow, & time after time you will bring
A little piece of happiness wherever you go.
Bruises, scrapes and cuts on your elbows, hands & knees
Are felt by those who love you and they wash away those
Great big tears with happy band-aids, a kiss, hug
And a smile or two from Mom or Dad even Grandma to
Right back you go without fear to do it all over again.
Written notes & drawings placed upon the fridge
In full view for all to see your special talents, bursting forth
Making it all worthwhile to see your precious smile
As all adore your wonderful gifts.
Time passes and school begins and an emptiness of
Silence ushers reality in and the pitter patter of little feet
Are no longer there to greet the rest of the morning
And now as your day at school begins the teacher
Provides a new way for you to learn more and more things
With Mom at home a moment she takes to steal a view
Of your room and the tears of love flow forth to know
The years are passing fast and every moment has to last
Longer and longer in the thoughts of our minds to know someday
you will leave the house and home you love
And start your journey, your path, your own life

Helpless romantic, guilty as charged

For loving too blatant, fast, hard or blindly
I struggle to believe anything, but what my heart
Can feel at this sight directly in front of me
I grow weak in the knees and
Appease every flowing thought of ecstasy that I need

I am, guilty as charged

It's something about this forbidden style that has me on fire
And pumped up, I can hardly breathe a moment more
For fear of bursting at the seams
Set adrift or tossed to one side of broken love
I have had many of these and yes, I have worn my heart
On many a pillowcase as well as my sleeves
For the intense passion I gave came from within
This heart so free to give all that I am
And I drop all my guards at random to proceed yet again

I am, guilty as charged

How little we know about love, yet we allow it to pass by
Right in front of our very eyes and see nothing at times.
Until we can grasp these incredible feelings & passions
Inside, hidden so deep and they do want to come out.
We are only lost souls like desert flowers struggling to
exist. That's why fate is the perchance to find the perfect
Mate we seek in every style of love

I am, guilty as charged

10 going on 25!

Truly there are times my parents never listen
To how I feel
It's not about the image they perceive
Or their
Personal feelings for being my parents and
Feeling threatened because
I was just being myself,
This is about me and my chance
To be unique
And develop my own personality
With guidance coming from them
When I know I need it
And yes I will challenge that too, that's just me
Excitement abounds inside of me
And I have to control it when I am around
My family & relatives
Outside I am a very different person
I can be silly, witty, or quite frankly
Just me when I am at school or with friends
I do get carried away and cause problems
For many a friend and my parents also,
Still another note is sent with me
From the teacher to them, as they need
To iron out the bugs in me again
Like that's going to happen
When I can't even do it myself,
I wish Mom & Dad good luck
Just kidding O.K.
Where's your sense of humor?

Empty window broken mirror

A longer route I now take to arrive back
At my temporary home these days
Just to delay what faces me ahead of
The emptiness inside those silent walls
That once were filled with very much laughter
And friendship
Although I know it will be a short parting
And this time too will pass quickly
But the silence I hear is very deafening these days
And I am weary, lost
& Counting my good fortune for new journeys
Plus I find myself watching
Many movies or chatting on the telephone
To pass the time until it is my time for sleep
Or just endless hours of non shopping
At HMV or department stores
And longing to reunite with my best friend
Yet, looking back before this
I realized it wasn't
That long ago I had spend most
Of my time on my own
Doing an endless routine that seems empty
How a mind adapts to the generosity
Of life itself and adapts quite well before
A little bell brings back reality
To a crashing halt right here right now
And shows us the
Necessary steps we need to take
In this our new path to endure idiosyncrasies

Violence is not an option just a copout

When your need to inflict pain for no reason at all & it is applied
just because you are stupid in your brain, doesn't give you the right
to carry it out with those who are frail or for that matter anybody
at all, you are a coward

Violence is not an option

Just because you want to, is to say at least pathetic on your part
and vile in all the eyes of those who see this & trying to shove the
blame onto that very person whom you did this to or others, is
deplorable on your part and leaves a bad taste in everybody's
mouth and you know it, so smarten up

Violence is not an option

What was overdue and definitely owing unto you as this
cantankerous ugly person inside is still a story as yet to unfold, but
it will follow & haunt you to give you your dues for the hurts you
inflicted. Violence is a copout on your part and a sickness within
only you and your soul

Violence is not an option

Doing unto others and laughing about it is shameful
And mean, especially when you use the ruse I'm
So frail you can't pick on me. Wrong you filthy idiot, life is a
special place to be involved in and most of us can see it from our
heart and soul, not you so remember violence is not an option it's a
stupid way out

When the trust is gone

Are we singing the same old sad songs for
Believing with out hearts or of long
Forgotten wrongs
Washed away are the fantasies & dreams
Everything had been replaced with their many-a
Well-planned scheme
Resistance to decision making with saying
That final farewell song
At the top of the charts, this is where
You belong
Brighten up that smile you once were so
Proud to wear
And paddle forward, now get yourself
Back into gear
It's in your best interest to carry on this way
After all it's a brand new day
Although your feelings have been hurt
Oh, by the way
In time they will heal
And you will have learned it wasn't
Such a big deal
Where do I belong you will say from
Time to time
And in all essence the outcome may not
Make any sense, reason or rhyme
So stop punishing yourself, it wasn't worth it
In the long haul
Take a deep breath, stand tall, look at your strength
Now you know it wasn't you that caused the fall

An ending

When an ending
Is an ending
As, an ending
Than,
An ending
Is an ending
As an ending
Should be.
Just allow for these
Judgments,
Applied
Gifts,
Journey's
For life,
Understanding,
Giftedness,
Bright futures,
Healing,
Strength,
Hopes, desires,
Happiness,
Wide spread learning,
So to, we can escape and awaken
These eyes
Forever.
And for now
We will deal
In life
For life is within us as we speak and in us as we breathe

A big bunch of misfits Pazzo, Pazzo

An evening starts and here they are ready to shake up anything
that comes their way with tantalizing conversation & scrumptious
foods for the palate.
It's an evening of pure relaxation and rebirth.
The people, place, aromas, amazing atmosphere
It's great because I feel this magic karma also
We are still a learning tool

For enjoyment is at hand and the best of laughter
Is right in front of you to carry on in such a gifted way
We can see life inside of life

It expels into this wondrous evening right from
The moment you sit yourself down another
Chance just to clown around in the greatest of
Company and after all what better way for you to unwind than
with contagious laughter and passionate releases of aimless
thoughts so appropriate for these occasions are
Splendid, simple, spontaneous, and free

You can feel it? You can breathe it each time you are there

With all hearts realizing exactly how they feel is
The time to share enjoyment with those you feel so open and
comfortable with
No judgments of comments just a gathering of empty
Thoughts and freedom of mind's expressions

Kick back relax as memories are made here today

By virtue of her character

She carried the weight of the day
Ever so gently within her path day by day
Her personality outshines her aura
Yet, so gentle, kind, loving, & friendly
Are the innocence from within
This soul of souls put forth
Unyielding from the tasks
And the visions
She has set for herself
Refreshing to the world is this
True character of heart
With strength to carry on
In respectful wonder and awe
Of all that surrounds her now and to
Move forward into her new journey
A walk of life's path
And the doors that will be opened for her
As every step taken, fulfills yet another
Chapter of growth, education, maturity
And the knowledge of passionate thoughts
To pass on to future generations of the excitement
And mind-boggling treasures yet to be experienced
Delights such as these
That set the heart on fire with gifted responses
Of another mind and talent which sets forth
A path previously followed just
Not quite in the same pattern
It's the concept we achieve with this walk

Caged beyond freedom of sea & forest

From the sea that surrounds life itself
That sustains us
Still your foolish brain remains as empty
As your coin-less pockets
Animals have rights just the same as you do
How then can you subject other life
To be a party to what they do not belong to
Let alone take them from their home
Be it the sea, trees, jungles,
Or other forests of life
How dare you make life mean so little
That you can stick
Any mammal, animal, bird or any other creature
Which is alive
In a cage, glass, or water enclosure
Then subject it to no life
Just the darkness of your selfish life
Which is for you just part and parcel of
Your greed and everybody accepts it
Give your head a shake for you and your
Cohorts are self-centered & heartless fools
How many of you out there are still afraid
To close your eyes and sleep in the dark or
Leave your doors unlocked
And your windows opened at night
How would you feel if your life had been
Taken away with your heart quashed at every
Moment, second, hour, or as days disappear
With no chance at freedom ever

Kiss me my love

For it's your lips I need pressed close on mine, as I close my eyes
for the very last time in this world, so I can carry your image to my
grave in knowing it was only my love for you, that kept me free to
dream and become all that I could be and I know I did so with your
support

Kiss me my love

As a lifetime of memories passes by so fast as I lay here with your
sweet hands pressed so gentle upon mine and I feel helpless as I
watch a tear fall upon your cheek, yet I am too weak to help rid
you of this pain you feel inside

Kiss me my love

For the moment is here and I do fear of an emptiness within this
heart that I have loved for so long, reflecting back in time on those
happy memories we shared, does little to comfort you now, but in
time you will be able to carry on and always know I am near

Kiss me my love

For my heart has beat its last and the light from above beckons me
to follow and as I rise above this body of mine a last look over my
shoulder I now take and place a kiss upon my palm and blow it
back to you
Kiss me my love for our love shall always be
Kiss me my love and let your emptiness start to heal

A Parent's Simple Wish with Love

I don't want to ever miss a thing you do as you start
This precious life of yours from birth, not even a single utterance
of nonsense said or spoken by you

A Parent's Simple Wish with Love

I hate closing my eyes as you lie there sleeping for fear I will miss
out on something so beautiful you did I could never feel it again

A Parent's Simple Wish with Love

Watching you grow brings every precious moment-by-moment
second-by-second hour-by-hour day-by-day more intriguing. I
can't get enough of how beautiful you are and seeing your
personality grow shows me your path is true

A Parent's Simple Wish with Love

Knowing the trust you have in telling me your feelings and sharing
your pain gives a warmth inside of me to comfort you through
these painful times and I feel very lucky to be able to be there for
you

A Parent's Simple Wish with Love

And whatever you do in life know I will support you in all of your
endeavors and trust your judgments because I love you and I
believe in you open heartedly

Seeking a Miracle through Faith & Trust

When the innocence of hope stares
Right back at your face through a newborn's eyes
Or a child's face
A miracle I see is needed here for these
Very special children
With different medical needs,
How can your heart
Not break and your tears flood forth
Uncontrollably for these
Precious souls
Of ones so frail,
A fighting chance to be as free
And live their lives
Just like you and I
Is all they seek, want, and need
For they are too young to state
For themselves
Their pain which they feel
Their many lengthy
Surgeries have come and gone
Yet love from so many is all that it takes
To help these young ones heal
And cope with life in a different way
And a constant bedside vigilance is now
Taken by those that love these little ones
Fear not for greater are the hearts
Of those who see you laying there so helpless
And they too will open their pockets,
Wallets, and purses so you can have that very chance

Write me a Cure to set my soul free

Oh help me blessed Jesus Christ
My Lord and savior, Redeemer
Through this frightening fog as my heart
Can't stand any more heartache, hardships,
Pain, or shame
Please, I beg of you hear my plea
Bring into me
Your divine power, glory, grace
And your heart to succeed
Do not deny my need for
A stubborn fool I will stay
And yes
On captive knees next to my bed
With my hands as rough as they be
Clasped together and head held high towards
Your perfect heaven
I focus my path on your way
Not mine any more
For you are my alpha & my omega
In this my human life
I will walk the light of light
Talk the talk of talk for you
And surrender my needs for those
Which you have called upon me to do
For it is you who put me here and it is you
That will remove me from this world
I am your messenger Oh Lord
Share with me now that which you
Need me to do

Confused words I babble

I can't remember what I said
I can't remember what I read
I can't surrender if I cry
I can't surrender lest I try
I can't lie in bed
I can't I'm sure be there dead
I can't allow myself to dread
I can't survive without my head
I can't concentrate with what I said
I can't survive without bread
I can't on what I pledge
I can't remember if I fed
I can't at all inside this head
I can't picture a sea of red
I can't stand this way and that
I can't stand tall and sway my hat
I can't see what I led
I can't see whom I bed
I can't keep working so hard
I can't keep acting as a card
I can't give thought nor deeds
I can't ever think of reeds
I can't fear others will
I can't fear when I take pills
I can't without caring for anything at all
I can't keep fearing I will fall
I can't fear your curse
I can't empty your purse

Dragonflies on a Warm Summer's Breeze

Hovering above me
As I lie here tanning myself are
Several squadrons
Of newly-hatched dragonflies
In perfect formation
They are ready to strike
And instilled from birth to kill is
This built-in instinct
Casually floating on air
Silently waiting and
Forever alert to their needs
& Surroundings
While they watch for the mosquito larva
To take flight
Ever alert in this hunt
For their prey
Yet, as the food chain goes
These mosquitoes are unaware
Of the events that will unfold
Watch now as a few of these dragonflies
Leave their formations
And drop straight down
Inches above me to capture newly-
Hatched mosquitoes
Then as fast as they dropped
Right back they go to their exact position
Section by section they drop and then return
To do it again and again

When Evening Nears

The day has all but finished and the dew sits on the waters edge.
It's time to relax and enjoy the night with a campfire
On my favorite beach and watch as the bats from their resting
places awaken and emerge swift of wing into their night, searching
once again for their evening meal
Without a sound their movements are
As graceful as nothing I have ever seen
This way and that way, back and forth they
Swoop, circle, and glide
Still only a glimpse we see of them as a shadow
Of darkness passes the reflective
Image of the moonlit lake in front of me here, right now
Sounds of the gentle water pushing itself onto shore
Brings a calmness to one's inner self
And welcomes so much more
A squirrel scampers in front of me and climbs
The big old tree, then he stops part way up and
Starts to scold me for being here
In this his habitat home
The mountains so majestic and regal in
The foreground are breathtaking as can be
With their tall trees and many colors of green
Placed there for all to see and feel
The beauty it unleashes with each passing second
All is quiet now except for the crackling
Of the fire and the sounds of a loon's eerie tune carried on a very
light summer-night's breeze

A Moment in Time

A hummingbird came to visit today as I was watching my daughter
who was staring dreamily into space on the sundeck of this
enchanted cottage on Mabel lake in B.C. and its length full beauty
hidden rustically back in the forest making it look like a fairytale
cottage hidden from view and romancing the eyes of the beholders
as they passed
When out of the blue I noticed a beautiful creature
Flying stationary in mid air just in front of
My daughter's right hand as she was holding
An ice-cold bottle of water
As he hovered so very close I could see as his head tip from side
to side, he was uncertain and puzzled
At the sight he beheld before him
He paused and moved back a smidgeon or two
Then before you could blink and quick as a wink
It moved sideways and landed on the tip of a tiny branch
Just a few inches away and again it tilted its head
This way then that way and as suddenly as he appeared
He disappeared between the trees
The very next day I watched as the hummingbird returned
This time on the clothes line was my daughter's newly washed
shirt hanging to dry, it has flowered patterns on the front and the
little hummingbird mistakenly thought it
Was real flowers as he tried to seek its nectar,
Flower by flower it searched in vain then when it had tasted all the
flowers on the shirt it paused for just a split second, this time he
just flew away never to be seen again
And a smile comes upon my face every time I think of that
Special moment captured in time and in my mind

A Box of Ashes
is all I have left of my Baby

How senseless is the driven motive to kill and the about-face
changes to those lives affected by those
Who choose to play our loved one's final song
This world of ours has changed so much in recent
Times, that society expects this, yet they still treat it as a normal
function of life as they see it
Kids killing kids will not and should never be accepted
By anybody and children have to be taught better, supervised
properly and directed with more solid guidance than they have
been previously given.
Respect, dignity, self control have been thrown
By the wayside and in its place is a gun which
They believe gives them the respect they seek,
But for the parents it is the sights and sounds of
Loved ones that echo no more in their homes
Only memories of the past shared with so much love, tenderness,
laughter, and friendship.
Gone are the times for sharing, crying, holding,
Special moments and helping them plan
For their bright future
All this and so much more has been taken away
In an instant because of stupid pride and far too
Many people thinking they are so cool and
Way too many people thinking they are big shots
And in the end they turn out to be just reckless
Losers wandering the wrong path with no future
Ahead of them except jail time, bad company, drugs, & despair,
open your minds, your hearts before it is too late for you, because
somewhere out there you know there is love

A Newfoundland Poet I shall remain

And my brain is like a new-born tree sprouting, majestic, mystic
with each brand-new day
For it expresses itself silently with every new quivering branch &
height it doth produce with tenderness, loving care, prudent selfish
pride, admiration, understanding and blissful adornment
You can hold your breath & watch now with amazement in those
eyes of yours for behold and see
As it extends itself for all of our eyes to marvel at, as its new
leaves proudly unfold and stretch themselves in this warm sun and
early morning dew of renewed growth and faith
As too do the thoughts of this poet blissfully express
A vision so full of renewed hope, life and yes
For all eyes to witness, see & marvel at the wonders this universe
has brought this way for you, myself
And countless more to see, appreciate, and thankfully protect what
you behold at any cost.
To bask in its heavenly glory is seeing and believing
Now heed my words and listen well for I now shall dispel the
problems not understood in this your thoughts from your head, think
not what comes from this writer's head, Better yet, what the
words say for you are the only essence it seeks and therefore you
help me speak of the mighty
Way-full expressions I feel and for others
Just how confusing it can be so,
Gather not your long-lost mind and enter in
To this that is divine and listen to your heart
For it bears the woes of not just your thoughts
But of your peers as well until this poem is understood

Time's a passage to keep us awake

Think about it for a minute
Stop what you are doing and for the first
Time in a very long time
Just simply listen

Time's a passage to keep us awake

And listen to our hearts and
Open our eyes and see that life
Is meant to be enjoyed by all

Time's a passage to keep us awake

How much are you aware of in these your
Present-day jobs or adventures
Do you know?

Time's a passage to keep us awake

How bold we are when we take
Everything for granted
And never prepare for the consequences

Time's a passage to keep us awake

And very honestly this only
Exists in our minds
As we are too afraid to admit our downfalls
Pity, isn't it?

Honesty of thought, freedom of mind

It's my mind and nothing matters
Except for teaching
Correct paths to those younger than you or me

Honesty of thought, freedom of mind

When was the last time you and yes
I mean you have simply
Gathered your thoughts to change

Honesty of thought, freedom of mind

Wasted expressions and failed breath
Make for wasted time
So change those thoughts & watch the changes in you

Honesty of thought, freedom of mind

A dream state exists in all minds
And opening that is still the same
Wake up and smell the coffee if you dare

Honesty of thought, freedom of mind

Sometimes it is a crime if you ignore pleas and forgiveness
Better yet, what if the shoe were different?
Can you shrug it off if that were you asking?

Honesty of thought, freedom of mind

How fast

Between the sheets
Lays an animal too bright
And calm
As it replies
In silent breath for all to hear
As it boldly states!
I am that I am
I am not like them or same
I can
And so you can
But you aren't
As I am
For I awake
So do you
And separate as real
From the unfounded
This moment I need to feed
For my hunger
Depends upon how I do today
It's an everyday
Experience
Of the very
Life we breathe for
Failure is not acceptable
Or greeted with
An empty belly plus
We will challenge
Our lives
With full strength to succeed

Confusion until read 10 times

One the eye
Of time
It's your
Tummy
Not mine
Difficult it reads
It's not
And
You find it hard to believe
Beheld is what
You can not see as was
What you tried
To perceive
The measure of time
Is never equaled
It is displaced because poetry
Is, I think easier to read
If the explanation
Is offered
Straight up for
All to see
Fear not
For the words you have read
Will stand forever
Within
All of our heads
And at any moment in time
It will portray
Your very soul

With the torch of forever

I shall always love thee though time may not be
Favorable or kind it's all in the perception
Of the ones stuck in our minds, full of ongoing ideas
And the concepts we want to share and endure.
Delicate is the heart when love enters in
And the gambit is well worth the risk
Once again to open wide this true path
You shall have to allow your flow to be free
Follow your heart and the feelings within you
And have courage to know true love is in the hearts
Of both paths that cross
Passions are bursting at the seams and it is
Welcomed with delight and excitement
As these two love birds are joined hand in hand
And run in the abyss of their minds
Voids are filled herein with life, smiles, & gentle touching
So much they have to say and learn about themselves
With open curiosity and willingness to believe
It is now their time to experience such romance
And set their paths as one together
Love is so revealing, sincere, honest & open
It allows us to float on clouds a-many
The world of love is at your fingertips and the
Passageways have just begun to be explored
Set your delicate love onto this trail of mystic beauty
And take time to stop from time to time and
Blend in your surroundings with that which you both seek
True love exists, it's just around the corner coming in search of you

Fragrance of love

Love is on the air and in the breath we breathe
It is sifted into our very essence as it stands
For one of the reasons we exist and are born.
Our souls are built
To withstand faded love again and again
Strictly to reveal oneself
Repeating that which is flowing
On the very next wave of life
And of swift showery rivers
Of excitement & belief
Corralling minute effervescences of thought
Expanding its weight for all
To marvel upon and move
Into fragrant wave lines of endurance
And enlightenment exceeding
Pent-up dreamy dreams as we sleep
Without awakening
We can feel this intense feeling
Within every part of our very soul
Of existence
And our minds are set ablaze
With this renewed curiosity, strength
And the way it survives
This is now the time
To give into that which
Is the strongest
Your desire to love
And to be loved

On shadows of your breath my breath & theirs

Screams from our hearts sent shivers into our
Very soul as death takes a foothold
Into what we call personal
For their life and final fight are now over still
Most of us find the strength to carry on
Despite the feelings and the tears
Plus all those memories that were mere shadows
Come flooding back full bore
Kindness from others helps to dissolve pain
And tunnels of confusion we are in.
So you see it's your continuance
With life that keeps those memories alive
Because of our loved ones that went before us
Would want it no other way
Sharing your adventures, experiences
Laughter, joy and peace of mind
Will continue to open the hearts of our
Dearly departed as they look down
From heaven and keep us secure and safe in
Knowing we will carry on despite an emptiness
Inside, but there will be brighter days ahead.
Take guidance and comfort in knowing you had them for so many
years and now it is your turn to walk on and grow into your own
future and every so often stop what you are doing and look up
towards our heaven and tell them from your heart, I miss you & a
garden of sadness will be lifted
And the skies will clear to reveal blue skies and clear paths for
sailing

Captivated in Awe

Listen now as the eerie sound of the flute
Plays its tune alongside the violin
And close your eyes and drift
Your mind's thoughts to floating over
The wind-swept mountains by the sea
As the two blend themselves so mystically
With the rhythms of the sounds,
And the sights drift freely with you
Look at all there is to see and
Mystify your very soul in wonderment
As the piano, harp, oboe, and wind instruments
Create their touch of elegance
And flair and gather the essence
With pride and a wee tear in your eyes
For the beauty of the land is upon us
And the melody carries its purpose and
Fulfills the heart of the earth and of ourselves
The tin whistle adds to the elegance
Giving its strength to wind-swept fields in Ireland,
Scotland, Wales, and beyond,
Heed the sounds within its messages
And flow inside the path for
It has created sweet patterns of
Adornment and vivacious loving thoughts,
Endure all and release the white doves
Of paradise to roam about
This beautiful land of ours
Gather now the breath of life inside your eyes
And find its peace there in you and your passion

The energy of youth

With the unending time of youth
Their energy
Seems like it will never end
As they while away the endless hours
Of play
Without a care in this world just
The supreme innocence of life
Flowing forth with effortless motion.
The sparkle
In their eyes is testimony
Of this and the faith, love, and trust in their
Peers, family, and friends
Are evident throughout their carefree
Actions, what they do and say,
Their thinking process is so refreshing that
We have to step back for a moment and
Blend our thinking process
To the way it was for us
Then we too fall back to times
In our past that delighted and
Excited us in just the same way
As that which we see before us today
And we get lost in the past for a time
To blend these two thoughts together
Oh, but never smothering
Are these moments,
Just a well-blended mix
Of pleasant emotional awes
And acceptance of personal joys and memories

Always a new look instead of the old

As I repeat Xin Yan
How creative and impressive are these words
That find their way into many-a heart
Open wide are the eyes
Of a true believer because
Fortune and fame are not
The glories they ask, just
A second to express and state
That which is unknown
Needs to be seen,
Researched, explored, inhaled
And savored for the true essences are
Held within the heart of the person
Bearing this name
Open your minds and expand
That which
You do not know and journey
Into this brilliant path
Of beauty
Life, passion and carefree existence
Now, as you absorb these thoughts
Open your eyes to the beauty
Standing right in front of you
And hold onto every glorious moment
You can before it has disappeared
Forever as a glancing moment
Throughout the process
Of our minds

The feeling from within

The texture of my heart
Resides within you
So powerfully
And driven by truth
The providence of reality
Is as a word expressed
This
Will be as
Natural as bees and
Hummingbirds
Seeking nectar
From the flowers of
Life, its time and balance
For a productive heart
Lacks nothing
And brings a wealth
Of happiness,
Hope,
Prosperity,
Joy, &
Freedom
To explore
Plus a wanton
Devotion to
Bring about
Others in just
The same way
Not by force
Just by faith

Reflective light
through an open mirror

Begins with what we see there lurking
As a pattern, symbol, omen, or worse
What then are you seeking or hiding from?
Can it be a lesson is about to embark
Inside of you to find its truth
Or an emerging image of what lies
In wait in your future that shadows
Your very thoughts and being?
Let loose those demons and seek out
The truth you have there inside
Of you
Do not think this goes unnoticed even
Though time had passed by as seconds,
Minutes, hours, months, or even years
The truth within shall & has to
Set itself free, for this pattern will follow
You into the future of younger generations
And they will believe it's the norm
As they were taught
Then how bad is the guilt you will feel?
Heighten the self control of your own image
As it is better to admit defeat than
To suffer the consequences
Accept only that which you can do instead
Of the false tongues that plague you
I guess the last line in this poem is now
Yours to finish for you have to be brave
And accept defeat and set a better way of life
For all that have followed your way

A rainbow's arc
over the autumn trees

Breathless sheer breathless how it captures
Everyone off guard each and every time
And the mist how it heightens itself
Above the trees to add an elegance
So mystifying we are all in awe

Such a wonder to behold

The heavenly brush strokes how appealing
Nurturing and revealing
Flow forth on a gentle breeze

Such a wonder to behold

Breathe in its glorious fragrances and watch
As the clouds more forward to reveal
From the shadows the vastness of colors
Stretching themselves beyond belief

Such a wonder to behold

As the rustic colors drift slowly
To the ground to release their nectar
Back to the land
For the beautiful greenery it had beheld,
Open wide this scene for it will be repeated
Time and again and with splendor

Such a wonder to behold

Blessed is the night

For it gives us a chance to ponder and reflect back
On the day's events, beautiful tidings,
Messages of rebirth

Blessed is the night

For the stillness in the air
Captures our ears & minds to magnify
Our beliefs into reality

Blessed is the night

For the holy one
Has sent his angles to stand
By our sides to protect us as we sleep

Blessed is the night

For the world we live in
Offers so many opportunities
To create new understandings and awaken
Within us our very souls

Blessed is the night

For a new morn will dawn
With invigorating renewal for us
To spread our wings and soar to new heights

Out of the darkness back to life

Though you may feel
Down in the dumps
What shall I do
Or say
To make you
Open
Your eyes
And believe?
Dream
Of good things
And
By the hand
Of God's
Almighty
Strength
You can
See
The total
Picture
Which he
Has
In store
For you
How then
Can I
Help you
To see
His almighty
Plan?

I will not bat an eye until I know

Your heart is pure and so refreshing
Like that of emerging rays of sunshine,
It blossoms all that it touches

Won't you let me in?

Like a gentle breeze sent forth
Its breath brings
New life to all that it passes

Won't you let me in?

And welcome in the morning dew
On yet another captivated
Peaceful day

Won't you let me in?

Hold onto those dreams
For a passion wells within you
And longs to be set free from its bubble

Won't you let me in?

And keep a happy thought
Throughout today and well into tomorrows
For a smile is more welcome than a frown

Won't you let me in?

Strength in knowing, knowing is the beginning

It's not what you say and do that counts
It's how you react
That shows throughout your life and it carries
With you for the rest of your life
And it's true. For the chance you get
Can change from one,
To a masterful number of two

Are you willing? I'll show you the way

Don't let it slip away,
What's inside of you decides
This truth and the journeys you take.
Molten lava is a reaction so volatile as that
Of some tempers and they too will eventually cool

Are you willing? I'll show you the way

How then can you begin anew?
Let's examine this which you ponder and show
Faith in the education you were shown
And clue in to a chance to start again
Open that rusty pulsating thing you call
Your heart

Are you willing? I'll show you the way

Pass not by the reality of the past, just stop waiting
Before it becomes your last

With a guitar in my hand

Tears in my eyes, my dog by my side
And my truck and bike in the yard
I sit here and write why I cry
A simple lesson or a bitter pill to swallow
Still sits in the pit of my stomach
And makes me ill to think of the time I have
Wasted on you and I am the only one to blame

Always country nothing less

My beer glass is empty plus
And my sleeves are wet
As another sad song airs on the radio to
Remind me of what went wrong

Always country nothing less

My motorcycle is ready
To hit the open road
And I better smarten up
Before the pedal hits the floor

Always country nothing less

And in the end it is all coming
Back to me now, so to speak
Do you get my drift?

Oh, how her eyes lit up

It all started when an angel came
To visit her and oh, what a sight it was for her,
Now you can see those angels thought her.
Are you willing?

Thank you Lord

Feel through her and grieve
Through her for we are the sinners
And Christ was her begotten son

Thank you Lord

For allowing a life so precious, exceptional,
Devoted, without revenge or malice
To accept one and all

Thank you Lord

Yet the world continues to be in a state
Of refusal, denial, brainwashed minds
Or corrupt indulgence in evil

Thank you Lord

For giving us your son so we can learn a better path
Through Christ and his life

Thank you Lord

Still searching for your own identity

Or

Do we already have one?

Are we still not quite there yet? Are we achievers?

Or

Are we just trying to find out where we belong?

Are we trapped inside?

Or

Are we confused about life itself?

Are we fitting in?

Or

Are we fooling ourselves?

Are we capable of holding our heads up high?

Or

Are we just afraid to try?

Who knows you might like what you see

At first light I see

On a gentle breeze the snow did arrive
This morn as it whispered
Its presence through my open window
A glimpse of this sight of snow I wanted to
View closer so I rested my arms upon my
Window sill as a flake lay itself
Upon my arm then it vanished
Into a water droplet so pure and clear
Right before my very eyes
This cool refreshing air
Stands all around as it entered deep
From my head to the tips
Of my toes
And a shiver reminds me
Once again, now is the time to put on hold
Any further plans for summer
Or fall outings and
Set my path
Onto new adventures
Into this great outdoors we have,
Soon the sounds I will hear
Are those
Of the young and old alike
Echoing their joyous shouts,
Screams
And playful attitudes
Will be skating, making snow angels,
Tobogganing, throwing snowballs
Or just having plain old-fashioned fun

Paradise
and its mountainous view

Oh, as I take in all this appearance
Of mountainous vivacious landscape
Before me
As presented throughout
The ages
And the panoramic scenery
It offered up for all
To marvel in and explore openly
I feel dizzy
And overwhelmed with excitement
For the passion of life
And nature abounds
With each step taken a new vision to behold
The clouds seem to say
Reach up
And gather me one by one
This one's for you that one's for them
Still the further I climb
The air becomes a little colder
I don't seem to mind at all
Up I go because I have in sight
A crest with snow on it
This journey in July has taken me to this
Most splendid of places
And I feel myself hurrying to get there
I see a spider at this height and little animals
Scouring about the mountain side
So busy and unaware of my presence
I love it all

A measure of a Life

Brought forward by bad
Stepping stones
Echos throughout the
Walls and
Tombs forever
A measure of a Life
Fought throughout the ages
And depleting
Is the demeanor
Of those left behind
Pleasant
Is the knowledge
To forge ahead
In knowing truth prevails
In seeking a path
Straight and true
Hidden
Beneath the past
Is the future
To start over again
Are you O.K.?
Now start to let go,
Step forward
Cast now that past
As that
Of shedding
A coat
From your
Shoulders

Timber wolves of Alberta

With their heads tilted skyward
And the moon so full, bright and clear as the sky
It shines its haunting light amongst the glitter of the snow
Yet, the wolves' reflective eyes are staring
Right through your heart, mind, and fears
For you are only food to them
Simple and plain
The eerie echo of their voices
And the sights of their warm breath shown by
The reflection of the moon, flowing on the air as they
Echo their howling voices throughout their domain
Haunts the shadows, valleys and trees with
Every single nook, crevice, and cranny
Sending chilling feelings
Up and down one's spine
Un-assurance enters your brain
As you tend to second guess your own self control
And struggle with the fears of reality
That try to enter inside your soul.
The chilling feeling remains
Within you so strong
Until you are back at home snuggled
And surrounded with familiar sights and sounds
In the warmth of your home and
Comforted in the safety of your bed sheets
That calm and reassure your body
With warmth, peace, mindful safety, and security,
But does this strength of ignorance
Drive shadows away?

Halloween Spook, Myth or Fiction

During our time
And going back to the 1600s
It's there for you to decide
Or are we now a culture that accepts
This weirdness, perversion of mind and
Exploitation of our young children's minds without
The fear and reverence of God's
Almighty power
Because we now teach this acceptance to the
Very parts of ourselves
And those are our children
Who make our existence worth while
Yet, trying to explain through the
Church's eyes or their way of thinking
Only shows they will go to any length
To keep you active in their parish,
Sunday school, or surroundings
For they are as well entering
The realm of norm
That Halloween is now an acceptance
Yet, the churches, clergy, & schools
Plan parties around this in an attempt
To sway your opinion
It is O.K. to believe or are you
Only trying to face your fears?

Empty of heart, who am I?

My life has been shattered by the words
Written and spoken by a child

Where am I after this, who am I after this?

Just a faded shadow without purpose
A silent wanderer of sorts

Where am I after this, who am I after this?

Drifting through emotions set forth with emptiness
And not knowing where to turn

Where am I after this, who am I after this?

Shock and humility have set its course in the veins
Of no recourse

Where am I after this, who am I after this?

Fighting back the tears to no avail as they set their
Journey downward on your cheeks
To the emptiness of the heart that awaits below

Where am I after this, who am I after this?

As the hours and days pass yet not a single call has
Been forthcoming and you wait there in your loneliness
Where am I after this, who am I after this?

A Junction where Sunrise & Sunset take place

Her absolute acceptance for this blessed purity for life
Abounds throughout her benevolent veins
Every morning, every night and is renewed the very next day
How shall we ever be worthy?
Through a kiss, a hug,
Maybe a silent conversation
I think not, but
Thank you, oh blessed King of sweet Kings,
For this blessing you sent to us is divine
So pure & true from her heart
And acceptance of this world
Will always be hers through her smile.
An outgoing personality
With such a thirst for life & peace
She can forge ahead from morn till night
How do we start to explore
Such a glorious perfection of womanhood
In this turmoil on life's difficulties
And un-forgivenesses in this world so tormented
But, she remains full of God's life blood
Vivacious, loving,
And so passionate for life,
That her endurance and
Caring for matters of the heart
Remains refreshing and
Without any iota of thought for reward
Just a single need to accomplish her
Hearts desires and to live life
As free and as gentle as a dove

Life, Love, & Laughter

What a concept, what a combination

From a single moment of contagious laughter
As it brings hearty tears welling in one's eyes
And shakes off the patterns of gray
Uplifting, consoling, pleasant
And so refreshing as the burdens of life are destroyed
And the weights removed from your shoulders

What a concept, what a combination

To the exhilarating passions of love
Brought back by the winds of time and
Forging through the veins of contented lovers
Lost inside of their visions for a future quest
Together hand in hand, side by side &
Year after year

What a concept, what a combination

As our world surrounds us with abounding life
And passages as yet untold and fabulous
Times awaiting for all of us to share
Gather now all of you that believe, for this life
Offers a spectacular oasis of knowledge
Handed to us from our highest power of all
And build new trails so the world can live
In peace and harmony will prevail
In the sunshine throughout your life

Teachers teaching Children

Just a reminder of how fragile and precious life really is.
How they teach them, will make all the difference in this world

Teachers teaching Children

Brings to light a moment to reflect on the important roles these
dedicated people bring about

Teachers teaching Children

Hallowed halls are reflected images of the past,
Present and future of our soon-to-be Einsteins,
Brought about because of their unselfish dedication

Teachers teaching Children

Open hearts, knowledge, patience, love and wisdom
For our children are their children of tomorrow
And they too bring the future

Teachers teaching Children

Stand up and take a bow for your
Time to shine, shall be now and forever locked
Into the hearts of those you teach
And we the parents shall remain indebted
To you and your families for the hours spent
Away from your own families to teach our children

Also available from PublishAmerica

THE DEBACLE
by Jeff Prebis

Buxxum, North Dakota. The town was named after its lone resource, Buxxum. The lives of the people depend on this resource. Without it, there would be no jobs for the people, no food on their tables, and no hope for survival. But what happens when the resource attacks? When every man, woman, and child becomes part of a diabolical role reversal that leaves no one safe?

Man has dominated the world for a long time. But now a new predator is on the loose that wants a piece of the pie. The adults are dead by daybreak. The children are missing, under the control of deadly beings. A few scattered survivors are left to sort through the corpses for fragments of the lives they once knew.

Paperback, 215 pages
6" x 9"
ISBN 1-4241-6583-0

Danny thought he had the world at his fingertips. He is a provocative painter who seduces the ladies of Buxxum and leaves them longing while he chases his next conquest. He is forced to do the unthinkable: to help someone else for the first time in his life. June has loved Danny since they went to high school. She finally has her turn with him and the world falls apart. Can she find him before she is killed? Can they escape the madness?

Martha is a simple schoolteacher who loves her son and longs to move from Buxxum to find a better life. They are separated at the outbreak of the debacle, and she has to fight against the gathering storm of evil to save her boy. Can she find him before it is too late?

Willy is a dirty little boy. Frequently he is picked on by his school chums. Will he take a shower? Will he put on a pair of trousers? Or will he become a beast that rivals the Buxxum?

Available to all bookstores nationwide.
www.publishamerica.com

CHRISTMAS SONG

by Suzanne Trammell

Pauley Sutton is an aspiring singer, but she needs a job. When she finds an advertisement for an opening at the prestigious Benson Group, she jumps at the interview, believing this may just be the break she's looking for. However, she finds out the job is more then she bargained for. The arrogant Eric Benson has other plans for his employee. Will she be able to survive this deceit?

Paperback, 73 pages
6" x 9"
ISBN 1-60610-829-8

About the author:

Suzanne Trammell was raised in the Washington, D.C., area but has traveled and lived in many different areas within the United States and overseas. Trammell now resides in a community in central Florida.

Also available from PublishAmerica

DEAR CHURCH
by Kathryn Cooper

Dear Church is the author's belief that Proverb 31:10-31, The Excellent Wife or Virtuous Woman, is in fact the Bride of Christ, His church. It is His call to excellence and was meant for such a time as now, to ready her for His coming. It is her belief that the proverb was not just a wise saying but a prophecy for today.

The author has taken the verses of the proverb as a guide to what the Bride of our Lord should be, especially for this generation. It is a message to the Body of Christ to come together under His headship as one body, one spirit, and one mind—His.

Paperback, 87 pages
6" x 9"
ISBN 1-4241-7310-8

About the author:

Kathryn Cooper was born in San Diego, California, and lived there until age fifteen when her family moved to Salem, Oregon. She attended South Salem High. She has three children and five grandchildren, and currently works as a revenue agent for the state. She enjoys playing games with family, fishing, and going on trips to the coast.

Available to all bookstores nationwide.
www.publishamerica.com